Help at Hand as Rushmore Cracks

PHOTOS BY NATIONAL PARK SERVICE

In aerial photos, black markers on Washington's face form a grid to map cracks.

SUMMARY: The four faces on Mount Rushmore are showing their age. Fifty next year, the Shrine of Democracy (dubbed locally) is getting spruced up for its anniversary, in all a $60 million repair job with park improvements. Watch for the granite quartet, which started as a trio on paper and was redesigned 14 times, next summer in its own TV gala.

George Washington, Abraham Lincoln, Thomas Jefferson and Teddy Roosevelt might be among the biggest names in democracy, but their sculpted images are not holding up as well as their reputations. Like many other 50-year-olds who expect to stay in the public eye forever, Mount Rushmore is getting a face-lift.

Cracks and fissures mar the mountainous sculpture. Thick white veins of repair run through noses, foreheads, mouths and hair. Although the cracks are not readily apparent from the viewing terraces and experts say the structure is in no immediate danger, monument officials agree the time to act is sooner rather than later.

The four-year, $60 million project already has begun with a comprehensive geological survey. When the results are in, probably sometime early this fall, efforts to stabilize, repair and preserve the mountaintop attraction will begin in earnest.

Subsequent phases will enlarge the small visitors' facilities, create a museum-like Center for Democracy, improve maintenance and security operations and complete the nearly inaccessible Hall of Records, a 68-foot-long tunnel near the top of the mountain.

Much of the money will be raised through donations from the public and corporations. And in July, President Bush signed the Mount Rushmore Commemorative Coin Act, which is expected to generate up to $37 million, half marked for the restoration.

All of this activity is leading up to a grand celebration of the monument's 50th anniversary next summer. The celebration will climax July Fourth, with an entertainment extravaganza featuring NBC News anchorman Tom Brokaw and "Entertainment Tonight" cohost Mary Hart, both former South Dakotans, as masters of ceremonies. And Radio City Music Hall Productions will produce the program for a live audience and for national television.

"We've learned quite a bit from watching the Statue of Liberty," says Jim Popovich, a Park Service spokesman, about the anniversary fund-raising for another American icon. "We'll do this right."

Even before 1924, when sculptor Gutzon Borglum, who was already known for massive works, was brought in to plan and sketch, Mount Rushmore was going to be *big*. Conceived as both a symbol of America's greatness and a tourist attraction (arguably related ideas), the environmental work was planned to put South Dakota on the map.

Rural educators emphasize the importance of
involving "the whole community in the education
process if things are to be turned around."

teachers will have to deal with deeper problems, including what Helge calls a "rural attitude" that permeates life in the countryside and is very difficult to overcome. The fierce independence that characterizes rural people often leads them to try to solve their problems without reliance on social services, she notes. It also makes them reluctant to turn to others for help, especially if they fear that confidentiality cannot be maintained. Another aspect is "low expectations for careers and life" that are bred from rural isolation, lack of role models and lack of acquaintance with the number of alternatives offered by education and training.

Rural educators emphasize the importance of involving "the whole community in the education process if things are to be turned around," Helge says. That notion is gleaned from the education movement often described as "smaller is better" and based in part on the work of James S. Coleman, a University of Chicago education professor who argues that school improvement is doomed to go only so far if it does not have the strong support of parents and other adults in the community.

Coleman calls the most important ingredient for success "social capital," the kind of intangible ties that people develop toward schools if they believe the schools are really doing their job. Coleman thinks so-

cial capital is particularly important for the at-risk young from poor and minority families, who are most likely to drop out.

A number of rural schools are putting "smaller is better" ideas into practice. At Rosman Elementary School in Rosman, N.C., for example, teachers a couple of years ago drew up "dream plans" for reforms they might undertake if they had the proper financing, says Principal Dawson Hogsed. Then they learned about RJR Nabisco Inc.'s Next Century Schools Program, which offers grants for experiments in education. They applied and got a grant for $750,000 over a three-year period, which began in August.

As many as 36 percent of Rosman students may be at risk, says Hogsed. The grant has allowed school officials to revamp the curriculum to take these students into consideration and to hire new staff.

But equally important is that the school now can offer classes that will allow adults to earn their high school diplomas, says Hogsed. "We know that at-risk students often have at-risk parents who didn't finish school," he says. Also available are courses

in such areas as secretarial work and banking as well as prenatal advice for pregnant teenagers and others.

Local residents with skills such as welding and repairing autos may be asked to teach courses in those fields. "By learning the skills our citizens have and making use of them, education is less divorced from the life of the area," Hogsed explains.

Even such an exemplary effort as this may not work, says Newlin, who points out that large percentages of rural one-parent families and families in which both parents work outside the home may hinder restor-

ing the kinds of bonds that once united families with schools. Still, he advises against pessimism. Courts have knocked down unequal financing in Kentucky and Montana and ordered that the great disparities between rich and poor school districts be evened. Similar court cases are pending in Delaware and elsewhere.

But the "great equalizer," says Newlin, is technology: satellite and fiber-optic programs that bring classes in subjects ranging from foreign languages to advanced math to small schools that could not afford teachers in those areas. "No longer will rural schools have to be apologetic about their limited curriculum," he says. Rosman Elementary, for example, added a roomful of terminals for computer training in August and has begun scheduling classes in reading and mathematics according to students' abilities in these areas, says Hogsed.

Another prime source of optimism is the resurgent strength of the rural education movement. Kinney's PURE, for example, which nearly died during the rural economic downturn of the early and mid-1980s, she says, has reorganized and is

planning for the future. And Newlin's NREA, which split off from the National Education Association 10 years ago to maintain its own identity, has risen from 300 members to 1,000, including organizations as well as individuals. Helge's institute is also growing steadily.

"There will always be a rural America. Everyone is not packing up and moving to the city," says Newlin. Education has "always been a long process of reorganization and renewal. We've been through it before."

— *Stephen Goode*

'White Hunter' Shot from the Hip

SUMMARY: Clint Eastwood's latest effort, "White Hunter, Black Heart," is a bungled rendition of a novel based loosely on John Huston's making of "The African Queen." The portrait of a movie director as a raging man raises questions — and doubts about Eastwood's acumen.

"Dirty Harry" goes to Africa.

I t is not often that a film as poorly conceived and executed as "White Hunter, Black Heart" comes along. That it was produced and directed by Clint Eastwood only makes the whole exercise so much more lamentable. But then, one has to admit, a number of years have elapsed since he did any work that was remotely interesting. His eagerly awaited film biography of Charlie Parker, "Bird," was weak and, more seriously, absurdly pretentious. The identical "Dirty Harry" movies he continues to churn out have become embarrassing to watch. Despite his extraordinary productivity over the past 20 years or so, his reputation is still largely based on his performance as Inspector "Dirty Harry" Callahan as well as on the first film he directed, "Play Misty for Me."

"White Hunter, Black Heart" purports to be loosely based on a novel with the same title, which itself purports to be loosely based on the making of the film "The African Queen." Eastwood plays the director, John Wilson, novelist Peter Viertel's version of John Huston.

The film, doubtless, aspires to pay homage to a great movie director. How does one do that? Certainly not by showing him working on the set from dawn to midnight.

Or by having him charm his actors and actresses into giving outstanding performances. Or by showing him getting involved at every stage of the production from the casting to the marketing of the film. Nowadays, according to the infantile minds responsible for most Hollywood filmmaking, greatness is all about having eccentric foibles. The tautology runs something like this: A great man is someone self-willed and obsessive. A self-willed and obsessive man will do everything in a self-willed and obsessive sort of way. Therefore, only self-willed and obsessive actions are to be expected from a great man.

From the beginning we see Wilson shouting rudely at his secretary, who does not seem to mind it one jot. We see him riding a horse at a fierce gallop, we see him getting into fights and receiving thrashings for his troubles. But his most self-willed and obsessive undertaking is his insistence that he shoot an elephant before getting down to directing the picture he was sent to Africa to direct.

Now, as self-willed and obsessive actions go, killing an elephant will probably strike today's audiences as cruel, puerile and pointless. "The African Queen" was released in 1951, and Viertel's novel came a few years later. Perhaps such an enterprise seemed more heroic then, or at least far less reprehensible, than it does in our much greener era. The script had been floating around Hollywood for about 30 years before Eastwood — for reasons best known to himself — bought it. Sensibilities have certainly changed during this time, which the film barely seems to take account of.

Nonetheless, there is scope here for an interesting portrait of a man whom we revere and yet many of whose ideas and interests, having been shaped by different assumptions, we might abhor. But that would require the kind of bold and imaginative movie-making that current filmmakers try to stay clear of. Consequently it will come as no surprise that Wilson not only never does kill an elephant but also comes round at the end to share our contemporary ecological prejudices. In which case, one has to ask: So what? So what that John Huston wanted to shoot an elephant — if, in fact, he did so — before getting down to shoot "The African Queen"?

If something of Huston's miserable experience went into the style or the substance of that film, then we should at least be told what it was. Otherwise, "White Hunter, Black Heart" comes across as an extremely unflattering picture of John Huston. Here is a silly, vain man wasting huge amounts of money as he undertakes a mission that no one has asked him to perform and for which he shows not the slightest aptitude. Maybe the film is suggesting that this was just one side of Huston. In which case, where is the other side? We never get to see him in the director's chair. Or, maybe Viertel, who worked on the script of "The African Queen" and yet is not credited with it in any of the reference books at this reviewer's hand, had a grudge against Huston. In which case, why would Eastwood get involved in such a morally dubious exercise?

But the film raises all sorts of questions about Eastwood's judgment. For one thing, his acting is pathetic. Wilson is supposed to be a driven, demonic tyrant. In Eastwood's hands he comes across as "Dirty Harry" Wilson. He talks barely above a whisper, he lacks presence and any sense of being a leader of men. Eastwood does not seem to have much ability to play anyone who is not a loner, an outcast. But a film director can never be that. Doubtless, Eastwood on the set is not Callahan.

But the weakness of the execution goes beyond his performance, even though there are virtually no other parts in the film. Richard Vanstone and Marisa Berenson as the Humphrey Bogart and Katharine Hepburn characters are walk-on parts. Jeff Fahey as Pete Verrill, the brilliant young scriptwriter, based on the novel's author, is just one long cliche. He gets to express the film's green sentiments about the killing of elephants (correct, as it happens, but heavy-handed and tiresome). But the script is perhaps the most disgraceful aspect of this film.

Viertel, James Bridges and Burt Kennedy, who wrote the screenplay, do not have the slightest idea of the way colonial society comported itself. There are also lines so gruesomely tasteless that one has to wonder whether all quality control has been abandoned in Hollywood. An English woman says, in effect, "One thing I did agree with Hitler about was his treatment of the Jews." That no one spotted how revoltingly inappropriate (and ludicrously implausible) this would be in a lightweight romantic adventure is a mark of the mediocre performances all around. Eastwood should be embarrassed to be responsible for, or even associated with, this product.

— *George Szamuel*

"Initially Borglum wanted a 700-foot stone staircase up here so people could view the heads up close. I guess that was before vandalism was prevalent."

And it has. The Shrine of Democracy, as it is known locally, attracts more than 2 million visitors each year.

Borglum was attracted to this particular mountain for its natural light and broad exposure. It was named for Charles E. Rushmore, a sharp New York lawyer who moved west to assist gold miners in their claims. Rushmore named the mountain after himself in 1885 and in 1930 contributed $5,000 as seed money to the memorial.

Lincoln, Washington and Jefferson were uncontested choices for immortality, and originally they were the only ones. When studies showed there was room for a fourth, Teddy Roosevelt was added to the plans.

Although the Rough Rider was considered by many to be too recent a hero for history to judge, he also was seen as a defender of the common man. President Calvin Coolidge backed his inclusion so enthusiastically that any true controversy was muted.

Although it seems as solid as the mountain it is carved into, the Shrine of Democracy evolved considerably in its planning stages. Initially Borglum wanted to depict the heroes from the waist up, but the unstable condition of the mountain and the prewar economy nixed that. At another point, Jefferson was on the other side of Washington, but the mountain could not support him there. There were 14 major changes in design from start to finish, not to mention constant tinkering to accommodate the unpredictable strengths and surfaces of the granite.

Completed in 1941, the Mount Rushmore sculpture took 14 years of blasting, chiseling, carving and sanding. It cost about $1 million, a combination of federal appropriation and private donation.

Workmen hiked up the side of the mountain carrying tools and machinery. They lowered themselves over the side with the same winches used by today's maintenance staff for the September crack-fixing ritual. Staff workers still use Borglum's recipe of granite dust, linseed oil and white lead.

Way back, behind Lincoln's head, the future Hall of Records was used for storing cable and maintenance equipment. A structural study will determine how sound the man-made tunnel is.

Borglum, born in Idaho to Danish immigrants, had hoped to house the history of the United States at Mount Rushmore, far away from the madness of the city. His family, living in Hermosa, S.D., is eager to see the project completed.

Workers in 1941 near completion, lowered by winches that are still used today.

"Initially Borglum wanted a 700-foot stone staircase up here so people could view the heads up close," says park ranger Mark Davison. "I guess that was before vandalism was prevalent."

Garden-variety spray-painting vandals would find it difficult to deface the memorial, but Greenpeace activists forced their way through security in 1987. Climbing up the back of the mountain, the environmental warriors lowered themselves from Borglum's winches and rappelled down the faces to unfurl a banner protesting acid rain.

The Sioux Indians, during their upheavals of the 1970s, occupied Mount Rushmore in 1972 and 1973. They camped for weeks each time just off the face of the mountain but did not disrupt daily tourism.

"It is very, very hard to take care of an icon," says Popovich, sighing. "Anytime anyone can gain something with those stunts — "

Yearning for "security from world affairs," Popovich notes that Ellsworth Air Force Base is nearby and that South Dakota has a large concentration of Minuteman missiles.

"Sometimes I think it would be nice to be Yellowstone Park or a glacier or something. Being the symbol of America, the icon of freedom and these values, . . . it makes you a target," he says.

Popovich reluctantly admits that terrorist groups have made threats against the mountain over the years, but he de-emphasizes the danger. "I guess we're lucky not to be in L.A. or New York," he says. "Just getting out here is hard."

That didn't faze Alfred Hitchcock, who was desperately disappointed that he was not allowed to shoot the famous chase scene in "North by Northwest" across the mountain's face. The director fashioned that scene with scale models in California, but Cary Grant's character really was shot in the dining room.

Terrorists and tourists are not the only ones with funny ideas about Mount Rushmore. Last year The American Spectator incited its readership to bombard the Shrine of Democracy with requests to add Ronald Reagan's face to the mountainside.

The idea was not received warmly. "It was carved to be a memorial to four great presidents, their ideals and aspirations," says Carol Reed, campaign coordinator for the Mount Rushmore National Memorial Society. "It's a work of art, and I really don't think we should mess with it."

Or, as Popovich says, "If someone wants to carve themselves a mountain, well, we'll show 'em how to do it."

— Betsy Pisik at Mount Rushmore

I

T HAS BEEN SAID that great aspirations are often contagious. Such was the case with Mt. Rushmore. It all started with another mountain Gutzon Borglum was carving in the South, the Stone Mountain Memorial to the Confederacy, an undertaking that attracted much attention in the news of that day. One man who read the newspaper accounts with interest was Doane Robinson, South Dakota historian. He invited Gutzon Borglum to the Black Hills of South Dakota to see if a mountain monument to America's greatness could be carved there.

Borglum *was* interested. Stone Mountain (which, incidentally, never was completed due to opposition to the project) had only increased his fascination with working on a large scale. He was challenged by the colossal. But, before he could give Mr. Robinson an answer, he must first make sure the proper rock was available.

Actually, what we were looking for that September day in 1925 when we arrived in the Black Hills was something more than a "rock". We were looking for a mountain—a very special mountain for Gutzon Borglum, *my father*, to blast and hammer and carve into the most magnificent monument mankind had ever produced!

But when you are 12 years old, as I was, or if you are an imaginative genius like he was, all things seem possible.

BASICALLY, there were four requirements Dad insisted upon; The stone must be solid enough to carve and to endure; it must face in a direction that

(Above) *Cathederal Cliff, Mt. Rushmore, in 1928 as the great granite face of Washington begins to emerge.* (Left) *Gutzon and Lincoln Borglum inspect the progress of work on the mountain. Gutzon delegated responsibility for much of the carving on the mountain to his son, Lincoln. The younger Borglum mastered all details of the work, including the complicated mathematics of transferring the measurements of the sculptor's models in large scale to the rock.*

would allow as much sunlight as possible to luminate the figures; the theme had to be important enough to justify turning a mountain into a memorial; and, lastly, there must be the will to have it succeed.

The mountain called Mt. Rushmore fitted the first two requirements better than any other stone. With guides and horses we searched the rugged granite upthrusts of the area for several weeks. The Black Hills are among the oldest in the world, and many of the great cliffs we examined were eroded, full of rock rot and had major faults. Mt. Rushmore seemed to be the best stone and it faced to the southeast where it would be in sunlight most of the day.

Scaling Mt. Rushmore was no easy task. The last 150 feet were almost perpendicular and our climbing methods would hardly have been approved by any experienced mountain climber. At one point we pryamided three men on each other's shoulders so the top man could loop his lariat over a projecting sliver of rock!

By such precarious methods we reached the top—6000 feet above sea level and a good 500 feet above all the surrounding cliffs. Only later did my father confess he was finally overwhelmed by the vastness of the undertaking. He later wrote:

"And it came to me in an almost terrifying manner that I had never sensed what I was planning—its dimensions...the vastness that lay here demanded complete remodeling of the grouping I had been dreaming. I must see, think, feel and draw in Thor's dimensions. The mountain was beginning to work."

The next question: what was important enough to justify carving a whole mountain? Dr. Robinson, my father and others interested in the project, including President Coolidge, eventually decided it must be a monument to this nation and to its philosophy of government, Democracy.

Rare photographs show (Left) the first ascent of Mt. Rushmore in 1925 and (Below) the placing of the flagstaff at the top. Pictured are Gutzon Borglum, his studio assistant Jesse Giles of North Carolina, and guide Ray Sanders (in hat) from Rapid City, S.D.

"Granite in this location erodes at the rate of less than one inch in one hundred thousand years. After I heard that I added a foot to Washington's nose. What is twelve inches on a nose to a face that is sixty feet in height? Twelve hundred thousand years, perhaps."

GUTZON BORGLUM

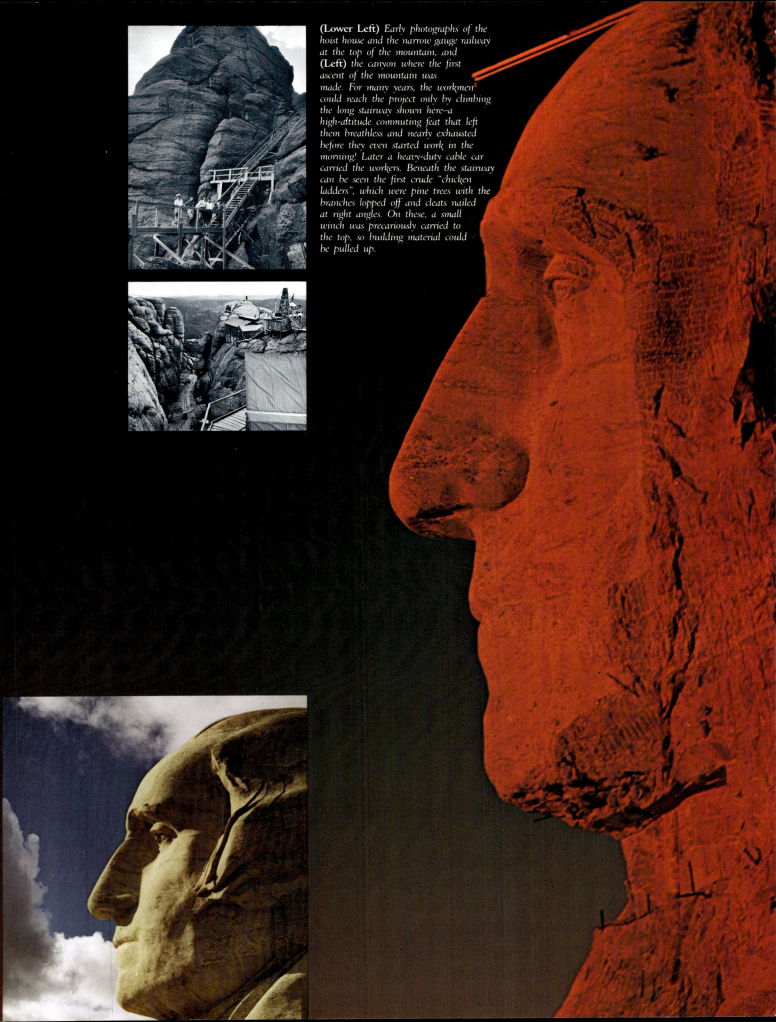

(Lower Left) Early photographs of the hoist house and the narrow gauge railway at the top of the mountain, and **(Left)** the canyon where the first ascent of the mountain was made. For many years, the workmen could reach the project only by climbing the long stairway shown here—a high-altitude commuting feat that left them breathless and nearly exhausted before they even started work in the morning! Later a heavy-duty cable car carried the workers. Beneath the stairway can be seen the first crude "chicken ladders", which were pine trees with the branches lopped off and cleats nailed at right angles. On these, a small winch was precariously carried to the top, so building material could be pulled up.

Nothing less than a masterpiece would do!

Frequently, the monument today is described as a memorial to our four greatest presidents–Washington, Jefferson, Lincoln and Theodore Roosevelt. Actually, it is a Shrine of Democracy, an imperishable record of a great people. My father used the faces of the four greatest presidents to illustrate this abstract idea.

The choice was not difficult: Washington, the father of our country; Jefferson, the author of the Declaration of Independence and the president who purchased the Louisiana Territory and set the nation on its westward course; and Lincoln, who saved the Union and extended the principle of freedom to all. The fourth choice was Theodore Roosevelt, who curbed big business and built the Panama Canal. He was also the only president who was familiar with the West and he had close associations with South Dakota. I remember that President Coolidge–who gave his support to the project in many ways–was especially concerned that Teddy Roosevelt be on the mountain because of his support to the labor unions.

The fourth requirement proved the most troublesome of all. The will to succeed was there, but the money was something else again. Private donations and collections from school children provided a financial start, but not enough for an undertaking that was to take 14 years, move over 400,000 tons of granite and cost nearly a million dollars! The State of South Dakota was not in a financial position to appropriate money. However, in the summer of 1927, President Coolidge visited the Black Hills. He became interested in the project and through his help Congress passed a bill making Mt. Rushmore a national

"Among the ancients, character seemed but incidental...The heads of the ancient Buddhas are little better modeled than a potato, with eyes about as open as a good mature potato. The Egyptian heads are more modeled and great beauty is shown but the method is artificial and the results are examples of craftsmanship in the age when the figure was produced rather than producing an historic document of the personality intended to be represented."

GUTZON BORGLUM

One of the Borglum family's stories concerns three of the workmen on the project. When asked what they were doing, the first replied, "I'm running a jackhammmer." the second said, "I'm getting $8 a day." But the third said, "I'm carving a memorial." He had caught a glimpse of the dream.

The photographs show: **(Lower)** *Thousands of feet above sea level, a workman wields his jackhammer from the special safety harness Gutzon Borglum designed. Buckled tightly around the waist, it was impossible to fall out of, even if unconscious.*

(Upper) *Borglum himself suspended in the harness. He often carried a small bucket of red paint, so he could quickly mark the rock for minor corrections in the carving.*

(Opposite Page) *Gutzon Borglum supervised the drilling which will remove the last few inches of stone on the lower lid of Jefferson's left eye. During the height of the work, some 400 drills were resharpened each day.*

memorial, appointing a national commission, and setting up a program that would match private funds dollar for dollar from the Treasury. A later law made the funds available as a direct grant because the Great Depression had literally dried up all sources of private money. But not before the work on Mt. Rushmore had been halted several times for lack of money to buy dynamite and pay the workmen.

BY THE TIME I was in high school, my father had his ambitious carving underway–despite a small setback from myself. He had completed his first design for the mountain in his San Antonio studio, and instructed me to put it in the back of the car and bring it to the Black Hills during my summer vacation. Unfortunately, I fell asleep at the wheel, rolled the car in a ditch and broke the model. The four heads came through intact, but my father had to make major repairs on the base. It also took three days and $100 to fix his automobile, which didn't contribute any to his disposition.

After that, my contributions to the mountain were of a more constructive nature.

In 1932, Dad lost his regular man and asked me to take on the pointing or measuring work on the memorial until another pointer could be trained. I did, with the understanding that I would do the pointing as needed, leaving me some time during the week to work at my ranch near Hermosa, S.D.

This agreement continued for the next two years– at no pay incidentally. My father was a persuasive man.

Finally this unprofitable arrangement came to an end in 1934. The work had progressed to the point where the full-time service of a pointer and an assistant were

"...I think we can meditate a little on those Americans ten thousand years from now when the weathering on the face of Washington and Jefferson and Lincoln shall have proceeded to perhaps a depth of a tenth of an inch–meditate and wonder what our decendents, and I think they will still be here, will think about us. Let us hope that at least they will give us the benefit of the doubt–that they will believe we have honestly striven every day and generation to preserve for our descendents a decent land to live in and a decent form of government to operate under."

PRESIDENT FRANKLIN D. ROOSEVELT
*at the 1936 unveiling of
the head of Thomas Jefferson*

(Upper) An immense American flag drapes the countenance of Thomas Jefferson at the 1936 unveiling ceremonies. President Franklin Delano Roosevelt was the guest speaker. (Lower) The rough face of Jefferson. Scaffolding was erected only for finishing work to smooth the stone to the contours of the face. Rough blasting and drilling was arduously accomplished by workmen suspended by cables over the side of the mountain like so many noisy, industrious spiders. Thus they could be quickly drawn up during blasting.

"The artist cannot escape his destiny...it forces him to leave home...to hurl himself against a gigantic rock, to cling like a human fly to a perpendicular peak, to struggle with a hostile human nature, in order to carve against the sky a record of the great experiment in democracy..."

MARY MONTGOMERY BORGLUM
wife of the late sculptor

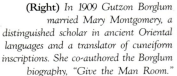

(Right) In 1909 Gutzon Borglum married Mary Montgomery, a distinguished scholar in ancient Oriental languages and a translator of cuneiform inscriptions. She co-authored the Borglum biography, "Give the Man Room."

Speakers at the 1927 consecration ceremony included (Left to Right): U.S. Senator Peter Norbeck of South Dakota; President Calvin Coolidge, who pledged national assistance to the project; South Dakota Governor William J. Bulow; and U.S. Senators Simeon D. Fess of Ohio and W.H. McMaster of South Dakota.

(Right) A workman prepares the deep drill holes for blasting.

(Left) *Gutzon Borglum with the first design for Mt. Rushmore. Faults in the rock required several regroupings of the four faces.*

(Below) *This photograph shows the Jefferson head being carved to the* **left** *of Washington. Shortly after this photograph was taken, severe faults were found in the granite there. Borglum had to blast the roughed-in face off the cliff and move the Jefferson head to its present location to the right and slightly below Washington.*

needed. The work then was getting close to the finished surface in many places and needed constant measurement. I accepted the job and went on the payroll as a full-time employee.

From then on I was in constant attendance on the mountain until the final scaffolding and machinery were removed—some nine months after the death of Gutzon Borglum. I had progressed from pointer to foreman to superintendent of all construction work; then, at the time of my father's death, I was appointed by the Mount Rushmore National Memorial Commission as Sculptor to complete the memorial. Later, I became the first superintendent of the area for the National Park Service.

THERE WAS NO TEXTBOOK on mountain carving; Gutzon Borglum developed the ways and means as the problems arose. There were plenty of the latter. In fact, as I look back on it now, the problems loom even more gigantic than the sculpture.

The greatest problem was to convince people that it should—and could—be done. There were no roads to the mountain, so materials and supplies had to be brought in by pack horses. Buildings had to be constructed—a blacksmith shop, a building for the compressors, a studio, a boarding house for the workmen. A donated diesel engine was installed at Keystone, then a virtual ghost town, and a powerline built to the memorial a good many miles away.

There were no trained stone carvers or sculptor's assistants available. Local miners were hired, which meant that every detail of the work had to be closely supervised. These were hardy men who commuted to their job each morning by climbing a sturdy but steep stairway hundreds of feet to the top, a feat which almost left them too exhausted to do any

work once they got there! Supplies were hauled up by winch; it was almost eight years before a heavy-duty cable car was built to carry the workmen, too.

Nor was it simply a matter of blasting off the stone that was not needed. It had to be removed in such a way that the stone that was left was not damaged. Under my father's exacting standards, the drillers and blasters became skilled stone carvers.

Engineering problems were met and overcome.

My father developed methods of working suspended from steel cables to such an extent that the men were free to move about over the vertical face of the mountain almost at will, carrying their tools and supplies with them. Hence it was not necessary to remove any scaffolding before blasting.

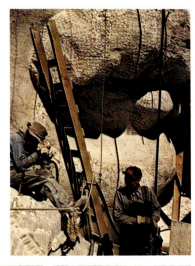

The arduous carving of Mt. Rushmore was performed at an altitude of over a mile above sea level. No lives were lost on the remarkable project, thanks to the stringent safety precautions of Gutzon Borglum.

Fastened into a leather harness or saddle, the workmen were lowered on steel cables from winches located on top of each head. A "callboy" was strategically placed where he could view both the winchmen and the riders below. The callboy ordered the raising and lowering of the workmen as they directed.

(Below) The final model for Mt. Rushmore, now housed in the new studio.

From these cables, the workmen removed the heavy overburden of stone by drilling deep holes and loading them with dynamite. (When you consider that the face of Washington is inside the original surface of the mountain some 20 feet, it can readily be seen that the task would have been almost impossible without the use of dynamite.)

The next stage was the removal of the stone close to the final surface. This was done without dynamite, so scaffolding could be used. Holes were drilled as close together as possible, then another tool was used to cut out the core between the holes.

At this point all the heads still had three inches of surface to carve. This we used to make corrections in the molding and allowances for natural lighting. Hence the lifelike–rather than mechanical– appearance of the four heads.

The final work was done from movable "cages" hung from cables. Air drills were used to drill in a honeycomb pattern at right angles to the final surface. Then the honeycomb sections were broken off by hand tools. Finally, the surface was smoothed with an air tool called a "bumper" which gave the mountain carving about the same finished texture as concrete paving.

The biggest construction problem was that the composition of the work could not be predetermined. Mt. Rushmore turned out to be a constant struggle between composition and finding solid stone for each of the four heads.

The mountain has four main fissures cutting through it at an angle of about 45 degrees and about 70 feet apart. They do not follow straight planes of cleavage, so the definite location of any of the heads could not be determined until all had been completely roughed out. Each was shifted several times.

As first planned, the head of Jefferson would have been to the left of Washington (as viewed from facing the monument), then the head of Lincoln and at far right the head of Roosevelt. A large panel with important dates and a brief resume of our history would have occupied the present position of the Lincoln head. But serious flaws were found in the stone to the left of Washington and the entire composition of the memorial had to be changed, resulting in the present location of the group.

It was then thought to use the other side

(Right) Lincoln's namesake, the Sculptor's son, who carried the project to completion upon the death of his father in 1941. (Below, Opposite Page) Other color photographs show the lowering of a wreath on Lincoln's birthday and the flag that draped the giant head at the 1938 dedication ceremony.

(Right) The eyes of Lincoln in this detailed photograph show how the Sculptor achieved the lifelike effect. The pupils are recessed–to remain in shadow–except for shafts of granite that reflect the light and thus give the eyes their remarkable lifelike glint when seen from the distance.

of the mountain for the inscription, but this plan was given up in favor of cutting a Hall of Records into the solid stone of the canyon behind the heads, and there carve the history of our country, the Declaration of Independence, and the reason for the memorial on the walls. The advantage of the latter plan was that the inscriptions would not weather and erode away.

Even during the finishing of the faces, the mountain still held surprises.

At the end of Lincoln's nose we ran into silver and lead, but not enough to interfere with the design. Washington's collar had to be carved with special care because of unusually large feldspar crystals. On Roosevelt's cheek, we ran into a red substance, a rare mineral called allanite. Fortunately, it occured in the hollow between nose and cheek and we could remove all of it as part of the design.

Accidents were not a major problem. It was one of Dad's greatest prides that none of his workers were killed or seriously injured. Our safety precautions were scrupulous. (He was not so careful about himself, however. Physicians said the strenuous high-altitude work of the carving weakened his heart and contributed to his death.)

There were some close squeaks, however. Lightning from a thunderstorm several miles away once exploded the dynamite a driller was preparing for a blast, throwing his cable out into space. Fortunately, as he swung back he had the presence of mind to kick the rock with his feet, keeping his knees bent, and avoided serious injury. Two other workmen narrowly escaped injury from the same lightning bolt. It was the last time anyone worked with dynamite when there was a storm visible anywhere in the area.

Too little of (civilization) lasts into tomorrow and tomorrow is strangely the enemy of today, as today has already begun to forget buried yesterday...Civilizations are ghouls. Egypt was pulled apart by its successor; Greece was divided among the Romans; Rome was pulled to pieces by bigotry...I want, somewhere in America...a few feet of stone that bears witness (to) the great things we accomplished as a nation, placed so high it won't pay to pull it down for lesser purposes."
GUTZON BORGLUM

In one sense, Borglum's masterpiece was unfinished. His original plans included a Hall of Records within the mountain. Work on the massive Hall was started, but for lack of Congressional appropriation suspended by the National Park Service shortly after the sculptor's death. Plans now call for enameled steel panels to be installed in a wooden box inside a steel box in the floor of the current Hall, in the center of the opening. The panels will have the history of the carving, along with a history of the United States. The boxes will be capped by a piece of granite, carved with a quotation from Gutzon Borglum.

Another near-disaster occurred when a steel wire controlling the hoist broke. The open box in which several workmen were riding came hurtling down. One of the men slowed the runway, however, by jamming an iron rod between the hoist wheel and the cable. One worker was injured slightly when he jumped out as the car hit.

Then there was the day one of the foremen, an Irishman named Matt Riley, got in a bit of a hurry. My father and I had to leave for a few days and Riley was instructed to take off a granite knob near the carving which detracted from the overall view. The usual procedure was to take the stone off in layers. However, since the knob wasn't part of the carving, Riley decided to drill deeply behind the knob and take the whole thing off in one big blast. We arrived on the scene just in time to see the massive knob shoot straight out from the side of the mountain. Then it began its thundering descent. It stopped a mere hundred feet or so from all our elaborate equipment and buildings that supplied the work at the top of the mountain. Riley was in disgrace for several days. Dad saw the humor in the incident, however.

THE BIGGEST ENEMIES of the

mountain are the old ones—moisture and freezing temperature. Moisture enters the fissures in the rock and freezing causes more cracks. When possible, the design took this into consideration so that any cracking would have a minimal effect.

When the actual work stopped, all fissures were sealed with a mixture of granite dust and white lead—a formula my father devised which has yet to be improved upon. Each spring the National Park Service lowers workmen over the colossal heads to check all fissures and again seal them if necessary.

OVER THE YEARS, one of the most

frequent suggestions made to me and to the National Park Service is that other figures be added to the group. There have been serious requests that considerations be given to Presidents Franklin D. Roosevelt and Kennedy. (There have been some not so serious proposals to add Clark Gable and other well-known personalities, too!) The truth is, it isn't possible. All the granite suitable for carving a colossal head has been used in the present design.

There is no more stone available on my father's mountain.

LINCOLN BORGLUM
died 1986

A MASTERPIECE in the National Park System...

*Each year approximately 2 ½ million visitors come to Mt. Rushmore
to stand and contemplate the greatness of our nation,
the immensity of Gutzon Borglum's masterpiece in stone.*

Each year there are more visitors than before.

*The Mount Rushmore National Memorial is near the geographic center of
the North American continent. Since 1941 the Memorial has been solely
administered and maintained by the National Park Service, U.S. Department
of the Interior. During the summer tourist season, rangers give hourly
orientation talks and a dramatic sculpture-lighting ceremony is held evenings
in the ampitheater.*

*Within the National Park System are over 375 such national monuments,
memorials and historic and scientific parks.*

These are our heritage, sounding over the centuries.